Amazing Retirement for the Nearly & Newly Retired

Focus on You and Your Life, Not Just Your Money!

Every day 10,000 people retire. After spending decades working, they are shocked to face the personal challenges of their lives' next phase. They need help!

In this tip-infused Itty Bitty Book, Mary Helen Conroy guides you through the process of retirement, to help you enjoy your bonus years.

Planning for the next 20 to 30 years of your life starts right inside these pages. Be prepared to challenge and expand your ideas of how you might live to enjoy your retirement years.

Are you ready to:

- Learn tips on making friends over 50?
- Embrace the changes of your next best chapter?
- Build a *life* not a *vacation* in your retirement?

Pick up a copy of this amazing book and begin to craft YOUR retirement life YOUR way today.

Your Amazing
Itty Bitty®
Retirement Book

*15 Essential Tips for You,
the Nearly and Newly Retired*

Mary Helen Conroy

Published by Itty Bitty® Publishing
A subsidiary of S & P Productions, Inc.

Printed in the United States of America

Itty Bitty® Publishing
311 Main Street, Suite D
El Segundo, CA 90245
(310) 640-8885

ISBN: 978-1-931191-81-4

Dedication

*For MD, for teaching me to play, helping me
realize my dreams and filling this life we share
with incredible love.*

*For all who hold my heart, thank you for being
an amazing part of my daring adventure called
life.*

Stop by our Itty Bitty® website to find interesting blog entries regarding **RETIREMENT.**

www.IttyBittyPublishing.com

Or visit Mary Helen at
www.lifesadaringadventure.com
and
www.virtualretirementparties.com
and
www.retireerebels.com
and
www.readysetretirebook.com

Table of Contents

INTRODUCTION

Congratulations! You are one of 10,000 baby boomers who will retire TODAY, or maybe next year. Let's start right now to explore how to make the *rest* of your life become the *best* of your life.

How did you come to pick up a book on retirement? Wasn't it just yesterday that you were in your teens and starting your work life? Wow, that seems like just a blink ago.

If you've picked up this Itty Bitty® book, you are nearly or newly retired. You've worked for a number of years now and reached the point where your life will no longer be defined by your title at work.

There are dozens of books about your money: how to save it, invest it and use it in retirement. That's not the focus of this book. This book is about helping you really LIVE your retirement.

How scary is that! Explore these 15 tips on how to make your retirement the best chapter of your life. Some may be obvious, others not so.

Tip 1
Let's Retire the Word *Retire*

Retirement is your new frontier. The nearly and newly retired boomer is smarter, wealthier, healthier and just more plain fun than retirees of previous generations.

We have lived through the social movements of civil rights, women's rights, and the new century. We watched a man land on the moon from our living rooms. We survived the technological revolution. Rebels in a strange new land called "retirement," we need to develop a new language of our own.

What can you say when asked: "What do you do?" Fight the stereotype of the word by saying:

1. "I'm retired from (your old field) and looking for new opportunities."
2. "I'm retired and not dead! And you?"
3. "I'm planning on retiring someday, but right now I'm exploring all my options."
4. "I'm the CEO of my life now. Want to hear about it?"
5. "Retirement is a journey, not a destination. Here's where I'm off to today."

Tips for Debunking Retirement Myths

Don't "retire"... re-wire, re-invent, re-tune, re-discover, re-define, re-examine.

- From now on, the years ahead are not *senior* years; they're *bonus* years. You've earned them, so resolve to live them.
- Break down the stereotypes: jog, listen to podcasts like RetireeRebels.com, start your own business, enjoy new hobbies.
- Forget how old you are: You know that you're only 22 in your head.
- Plan to maximize how you spend your *life* in retirement, not just your *money.*
- Life is a daring adventure, and you're not done yet! Enjoy these bonus years.
- Don't pine for the good old days that really never were. You are a survivor.
- Don't retire; instead, be selfishly employed in doing only what *you* want to do. Whatever that is.
- Old dogs and old people *can* learn new tricks. Grandma Moses started painting at age 78. Your life is what you make it.

Tip 2
No More Alarm Clocks!

Retirement's paradox is that there is so much time – and yet so little time. The best news about your choices is that they're not forever. You can always change your mind.

1. What's the focus of your retirement?
   a. **Service** – Volunteering, church work, vet work, service clubs, mentoring.
   b. **Recreation** – Marathons, fitness, photography, golf, knitting, baking.
   c. **Employment** – Part-time job, entrepreneur, turning your hobby into a source of revenue.
   d. **Family** – Childcare for grandchildren, care-giving for a partner or parent(s).
   e. **Travel** – RV living, snow birds, the 50 states challenge, visiting friends or relatives.
2. Do you know what you want to do?
   a. Have you made a bucket list?
   b. How do you see your ideal day?
   c. What world problem would you like to work toward resolving?
   d. Have you created a vision or life board to capture your ideas?

Resources to Help Find Your New Life Plan

- Volunteer. Check out <u>volunteermatch.com.</u>
- Serve a vet. Visit <u>serve.gov</u> and search the keyword "veterans."
- Visit your local senior center to check out its programs and services. You'll be amazed at the extent and variety.
- Join others in a new sport, activities like cooking or taking new classes.
- Visit your local library. The world is within its doors. From film festivals to Friends of the Library groups, to reading to children.
- Become an encore entrepreneur. Visit the <u>Small Business Association</u> or <u>SCORE</u> in your area.
- Create a bucket list. First, watch the movie *The Bucket List* (2007), then create your own on paper or online at <u>www.bucketlist.org.</u>
- Travel and learn through <u>roadscholar.org</u> or adventure travel with <u>eldertreks.com</u>

Tip 3
Taking The Next Step(s)

Successful aging is up to you. So what are you going to choose? Are you going to pull up a rocking chair and watch TV in the upcoming years? Or are you going to ditch the rocking chair and reinvent your bonus years to be your best years?

Key elements of your next step:

1. A sense of purpose
2. Connections with others
3. Personal growth
4. Self-acceptance
5. Autonomy
6. Health

Questions to Help Choose Your Next Step

- What gives your life meaning?
- Are you isolated or meeting new people?
- Do you look in the mirror and say, "Wow you're amazing today!"
- Do you have regrets? If so, what if anything are you going to do about them?
- Are you glad you were born?
- What have been the most defining moments in your life? What did you learn?
- Do you lead your own life or let others?
- Will your health affect your future?
- What might your 90-year-old self say about how you're spending these bonus years?

Tip 4
What's Your Adrenaline Drug?

In many ways, retirement is like having Post Traumatic Stress Disorder (PTSD). Each of us has different triggers for what gives us energy. Get to know yourself. What do you value?

1. **Do you seek stability and hard work?** Do you always see playing as earned only after work? Did you have support staff to rely on at work? Your adrenaline came from *being in charge*.
2. **Are you an independent thinker?** Do you like to explore ideas, build models to innovate? Your adrenaline comes from *information*.
3. **Are you driven by serving others?** Were you in a service industry? Is your working on a team important? Your adrenaline comes from *social interaction*.
4. **Are you always multi-tasking?** Do you prize freedom above all else? Do you like to do your own thing? Your adrenaline comes from *risk-taking*.

Exercises to Get to Know Yourself Better

- Talk to your friends, family and others who know you well. Interview them and ask them what they think makes you unique. Write down key phrases they use to describe you.
- Do a values assessment. What are the things that you treasure above all else?
- "Who am I?" is the quintessential question. You're not a job title. What makes you unique?
- What are your major likes and dislikes? What do you do that makes time disappear?
- Know your limits. Do you have any? Are they mental, financial, physical, emotional?
- Know your personality, found by Googling "personality tests." Each will provide you with a little more self-knowledge.
- Journal. Keeping a diary or a journal to record your current thinking is priceless. It can record your thoughts and help you to lay out a road map for your future.

Tip 5
Review, Retreat, Reinvent

If you google "retirement," you'll find tons of plans to assist you with your money. Most advertisements assure you that you don't have quite enough to live your dreams of non-working.

It wasn't money that concerned me the day I left my last career job. It was the growing angst in my heart. I knew I needed a reinvention. Have you ever felt that way? The same old situation creates the same old responses. In a way, I was glad the door was locked, to force me to begin again. I needed some new tools.

1. **The Tool of Review.** We need to *Re-View* our life to see what might be possible. What did we really always want to do? What is your unique talent?
2. **The Tool of Retreat**. Take time away from all you know. Withdraw from the world and allow yourself to design your future. *Re-treat* yourself with fun and discovery.
3. **The Tool of Reinvention.** Become a spaghetti maker; throwing new ideas up on the wall to see what sticks. *Re-Invent* every part of your life.

Exercises for the 3R's of Retirement

Review your life:
- Create a timeline of your life. What were you doing at age 5, 10, 16, 25, 45, now?
- Who were your mentors?
- What did you learn at each point?
- What did you enjoy doing?
- Look for the themes that created your unique life tapestry.

Retreat to re-examine your life
- Take a vacation or stay-cation, all by yourself.
- Reflect on the good, the bad and the amazing things you discovered in your review.

Reinvent your life
- Who will you be in retirement?
- What themes from your earlier life might create a framework for your new life in retirement?

Tip 6
Cultivate The Right Mindset

We're all creatures of habit, aren't we? We say the same things to ourselves day in and day out. That's what forms our memories and our cranial pathways. On some level, that's a good thing. It allows us to get out of bed, make coffee and drive to the bank without thinking. We constantly tell ourselves the same stories, give ourselves the same directions.

1. **Watch your language!**
    a. Did you know that we have between 12,000 and 60,000 thoughts per day?
    b. About 98% of them are the same ones we had yesterday.
    c. About 80% of those are negative.

2. **Watch your mindset!** (Dweck, 2006)
    a. *Fixed Mindset*. You are who you are. You try to avoid challenge and failure by doing the same thing all the time.
    b. *A Growth Mindset*. You are a work in progress. You are a blank canvas every morning, ready for new creations.

10 Exercises to Play the Growth Mindset Game:

- *What if I* tried a new radio station?
- *What if I* took a different route home?
- *What if I* learned to play pickle ball?
- *What if I* slept on the other side of the bed?
- *What if I* wore only red today?
- *What if I* walked 10,000 steps?
- *What if I* watched YouTube™ to learn about Facetime?
- *What if I* listened to podcasts like RetireeRebels™?
- *What if I* wrote a love letter?
- *What if I* stopped saying, "I can't"?

The biggest bully we'll ever meet is right in the mirror. Listen to what you say to yourself. Would you speak like that to someone you love?

Tip 7
Gray Divorce
("Til Retirement Do Us Part?")

What began so many years ago with the "til death do us part" phrase now needs to be amended to "or until retirement."

Called the "gray divorce," more and more senior couples just can't imagine spending their next 20 or 30 years together following their retirement.

1. Between 1990 and 2010, the divorce rate for those aged 50 and older has more than doubled. (U.S. Census) from 5 to 11 per thousand.
2. 48% were from first-time marriages. (U.S. Census)
3. Of those divorces, 66% were initiated by the wife. (AARP)
4. Stay-at-home mothers who hung in there for the children are now in their early 60s and many want to spread their wings.
5. Newly retired women and men report the lowest rate of marital satisfaction and the highest rate of marital conflict.

Tips to Staying Together

- Manage expectations. Understanding what each partner expects of the other can help ward off disappointments.
- Pursue your own interests and maintain some separate friendships. Establishing your own identity is good for personal growth.
- Select separate territories in the home. Choose your own pursuits and hobbies, and do these in your own area.
- Don't expect your partner to be with you on the couch, watching only what you love. Share the remote.
- Separate houses, separate sleeping rooms. Of senior couples, 35% sleep apart. Some plan date nights together!
- Know that you are not alone. Most happily married couples run into obstacles. It's not a reflection on you, and your marriage isn't necessarily falling apart. The key is how you resolve the issues.

Tip 8
Fun: The 'F' Word to Enjoy

When was the last time you had fun? Hope it was today. Fun is defined as the pleasure you discover in being distracted from a serious task. It's the enjoyment of taking pleasure in activities that just make you feel good.

1. Having fun is just a mindset, an attitude that it's ok to relax and even be a little silly.
2. Fun can be anywhere, not just on vacation. It can be dancing to your favorite tunes while doing the dishes.
3. Fun can take us away from what seems serious and necessary. Fun reminds us that we are all really kids in older bodies.
4. If you want to have fun, get into the right mindset and embrace every opportunity for a good time. If you're relaxed and not afraid to be a little silly, then you can have fun almost anywhere, at a party or in the middle of a laundry day.

Tips on having FUN

- Develop a new skill. Learn how to speak Japanese and try it out on the cat.
- Choose an indoor game and an outdoor game that you enjoy. Do them!
- Listen to music. Dance doing the laundry or sing karaoke loudly while vacuuming.
- Join EscapeAdulthood.com. It's the cure for the common life, helping you to break free from the clutches of *Adultitis*.
- Practice Laughing Yoga. Try to giggle seriously ten minutes every day.
- Plan your perfect vacation. Just planning it tells your brain that you're doing it!
- Try geocaching. Scavenger hunts in your own neighborhood can be interesting.
- Take $5 to spend as a visitor in your city.
- Go to a park and swing. Go to a zoo and pet. Go to a children's museum and play.

Tip 9
Your Encore: Entrepreneurship?

You've been working for someone else for most of your work life. Perhaps your retirement years will now make you a CEO. Become an encore entrepreneur.

1. Nearly one-quarter of all new businesses are started by those aged 55-64.
2. Ageism is rampant. Why face the rejection letters of seeking a new position? Create your own company.
3. Start small while you are still working, then build your business as you get closer to retirement.
4. Be computer savvy. Online, one can't see what you look like or how old you are. Create your website to sell your products or services.
5. Remember the lifetime of experience you bring to your new business.
6. Wish you knew how to do something like marketing, accounting, etc.? Take a class or find a partner. Two heads can be better.

Are You an Entrepreneur?

- What hobby or passion might you turn in to an encore business?
- Network for connections. Network for money. Network for information.
- You're older and wiser. You know a better way; you have the knowledge to make a difference. Create it, share it.
- Contact the Small Business Administration for tips, advisors and funding ideas.
- Can you multi-task well? Do you have a broad business background from PR to accounting? Put them to work.
- Are you comfortable taking risks?
- You're never too old to start your own business! Don't waste any more time.

Tip 10
"Ya Gotta Have Friends"

Remember all the friends you had: neighborhood pals, school chums, parenting buddies, work colleagues. Now you will have more time to look around. You want someone to play with again, and no one is there. Loneliness affects one in five retirees, so "Ya Gotta Have Friends!"

The Value of Friendship

1. **Companionship.** Life is always better together.
2. **Conversations.** Talking with a friend may be a simple Facebook™ post to an evening of chatting.
3. **A Helping Hand.** A friend has your back in good times and bad.
4. **Laughter.** Friends know what you'll think is funny.
5. **Advice.** A friend can help to provide a reality check and see different ways to look at your problems.

Tips for Finding a Friend

- **Ask yourself:** "Why do I want a friend?"
- **Ask yourself.** "What qualities should my new friend have?"
- **Join something!** Join a church group, a Scrabble game at the park, a book club, volunteer, or check out Meetup.com.
- **50 cups of coffee/tea/wine/water.** Invite someone for your favorite drink. No agenda, just talk.
- **Have a dinner party, a game night, a movie night.** Invite two people and have each bring someone new.
- **Take a class.** Being in a classroom of people wanting to learn the same thing creates an immediate connection.
- **Walk out your door.** A friend won't just appear. You have to put forth the effort.
- **Say "Yes!"** to everything, whether or not it's interesting to you. You might have found a new interest—and friend.

Tip 11
Move: Stretch Your Muscles

We've all heard that exercise is great for staying healthy in retirement. So maybe you would like to take a 100-mile bike ride or perhaps be a triathlete. You go! More and more seniors are stretching their bodies in just this way.

For others, moving the body is not only adding candles to the cake but adding life to those years. You look better, feel better, and have more energy. Moving your body moves your life and gives you a greater sense of well-being.

1. Exercise helps adults to maintain or lose weight.
2. Exercise reduces the effect of illness and chronic disease.
3. Exercise enhances mobility, flexibility and balance in older adults.
4. Exercise improves your sleep.
5. Exercise boosts mood and self-confidence.
6. Exercise is amazingly good for the brain.

Cornerstones of Fitness as You Age

Cardio
- Uses large muscle groups. Take a walk, climb stairs, play tennis, dance 20 minutes a day.

Strength and power
- Use free weights or elastic bands to build muscle.

Flexibility
- Develop your full range of motion. Yoga and Pilates are excellent for this.

Balance
- Maintain stability. Try yoga or Tai Chi.

Walking
- Moving the body through walking builds all the muscles. Try to walk 10,000 steps each day or for 30 minutes.

Mental Exercise
- Keep learning. Play computer games, Sudoku, crosswords. Keep stretching your brain muscles.

Find something you enjoy and resolve to move your body and mind every day!

Tip 12
What Did You Learn Today?

When was the last time you were so engrossed in learning something that the time flew by? You enjoy the luxury of allowing yourself to not scan a piece of information, but to truly fit the pieces of learning together in your head, just for you.

1. **Be curious.** Retirement gives you the time to be eager to learn anything.
2. **Invent**. Have you always wanted to create a new product, a new website, a new recipe?
3. **Enhance a skill.** Build on what you know, get better at something just for you.
4. **Keep the brain synapsing**. Using your mental skills today keeps you from losing them tomorrow.
5. **Go back to school.** You're never too old; teachers appreciate the wisdom that seniors can provide to the class.

Tips to Keep Learning

- **Develop your own Individual Personal Learning Project.** Make a plan to learn!
- **The Public Library.** The "people's university" is just a card away. Join the Friends of the Library. Join a book club. Read to children.
- **Park and Recreation Programs.** When was the last time you looked at the flyer that probably comes in your mailbox?
- **University Courses.** Classes can be taken face-to-face, online or by mail these days. Seniors usually receive a discount, and often you can audit classes for free.
- **RetireeRebels.com** See how you can become a 'certified' Retiree Rebel.
- **The Internet.** If you're not yet computer savvy, LEARN. From Google to YouTube.com, the world is yours.

Tip 13
Reclaim Your Creativity

Are you the artist of your own life? Creative activity can foster a sense of competence, purpose and growth. *Creative* might never have been a way to describe yourself; now you can start looking at new things that you might want to try. Being retired means that you now have time:

1. Time to (re)discover what makes you the creator of your own life.
2. Time to (re)discover what brings you joy.
3. Time to (re)define what spurs your creative juices.
4. Time to (re)discover your creativity; it enables your heart to sing, your head to explore, your hands to build and your senses to inhale the world around you.
5. Time to (re)discover what you always said you'd like to try.
6. Time to (re)discover what new adventures you could pursue.
7. Time to (re)discover how to weave your retirement into a tapestry of yourself.

Tips to Find Your Creativity

Are you a writer?

- Journal every day.
- Sign up for a writing course.
- Become an <u>Itty Bitty</u>® Publishing author.
- Write poetry.
- Work in a bookstore.

Are you a visual artist?

- Buy an adult coloring book, markers or a 64-box of crayons.
- Learn to quilt.
- Take a painting course.
- Go to an art store and explore.
- Visit a museum.
- Take a photography class.

Are you a musician?

- Take lessons on the instrument you always wished you could play.
- Buy a ukulele.
- Join a community group of singers or players.
- Get tickets to your local symphony.
- Find an open-mic night in your area.

Tip 14
What's Your Legacy?

The word *legacy* generally means receiving money or items from someone who died. It has been said that a true legacy is etched into the minds of others and the stories they share about you. It's leaving the lessons of your life to the future, not necessarily your gold. They can include:

1. Financial legacy
2. Family legacy
3. Medical legacy
4. Service legacy
5. Mentoring legacy
6. Perspective legacy

What's your legacy? What can you do to make sure it truly represents yourself when you're gone?

Questions for Thinking About Your Legacy

- Does your will reflect your current wishes? Have you named those who you want to remember? Who gets the pearls?
- Legacy planning can also include trusts and a durable power of attorney for health matters. Are these in place for you?
- Have you written out your own family history? Have you written a letter to your closest family members to be opened upon your death?
- Have you written your medical history to assure that your children have a record?
- Whom and what have you served in your life? Was it the humane society, your church or community?
- Whom have you mentored? How have you shared your talents and gifts with others?
- It's not too late to affect your legacy.

Tip 15
Ready, Set, Retire

It's time to retire. Whether you're 50 or 80, it is time to take the leap into the next chapter of your life. You'll never really be ready. Were you ready when you got married or became a parent? Like retirement, those have a framework but the details will be unique for each of us.

Retirement is only a transition:

1. Planning it all out: Euphoria.
2. Saying good-bye: Party and farewells.
3. Honeymoon Phase: I'm free.
4. Disillusionment: Is this all there is?
5. Reinvention: Designing the new you.
6. Moving on: The new everyday.

Tips for the Stages of Retirement

- Plan your retirement life. Use your imagination.
- Acknowledge your accomplishments. <u>Have a party</u>, take a vacation, celebrate your past life chapters.
- Sleep, without an alarm clock. You have years and years of sleep deprivation to replace. Take naps without shame too! Research indicates that 7-8 hours of sleep a night can ward off Alzheimer's disease.
- Are you bored or depressed? You're not alone; life as you've known it is different. Talk to folks and seek help if you need it.
- Be creative with your life. Try new things. Try old things again in a new way. Nobody is your judge.
- New routines become the new norm. Thrive in retirement on your terms.
- Remember, "Life's a Daring Adventure!" and you're not done yet! Enjoy YOUR retirement.

You've finished. Before you go...

Tweet/share that you finished this book.

Please star rate this book.

Reviews are solid gold to writers. Please take a few minutes to give us some itty bitty feedback.

ABOUT THE AUTHOR

Mary Helen Conroy is an encore (after her career life) entrepreneur, starting three companies working with the nearly and newly retired. Her bonus years are full; *speaking, writing, coaching, podcasting* and *giving virtual retirement parties.*

She is an adventurer extraordinaire. Enjoying the adventures of Nancy Drew at age 10 led her to a career in librarianship, teaching and sales.

Life is a daring adventure for her. She lives each day in Madison, WI, filled with the love of an amazing partner, family and friends.

A perfect stage for retirement…some day!

You can reach Mary Helen at:

www.lifesadaringadventure.com
and
www.virtualretirementparties.com
and
www.retireerebels.com
and
www.readysetretirebook.com

If you enjoyed this Itty Bitty® book you might also enjoy…

- **Your Amazing Itty Bitty® Empty Nesters Survival Handbook** – Dr. Dorine Kramer

- **Your Amazing Itty Bitty® Sexuality For Seniors Book** – Randy and Rev. Jenny Dickason

- **Your Amazing Itty Bitty® Staying Young At Any Age** – Dianna Whitley

Or any of our other Itty Bitty® books available online.

40889786R00028

Made in the USA
Middletown, DE
26 February 2017